Christmas Fun
songs and activities for children

Contents	page
Away in a manger	2
Silent night	4
Rudolph the red-nosed reindeer	6
When Santa got stuck up the chimney	8
Sticker fun!	10
O Christmas tree!	12
The twelve days of Christmas	14
We three kings	16
Frosty the snowman	18
Sticker fun!	20
Picture Dictionary	22
Answers	24
Jigsaw cut-out	25
Pop-up card	27
Christmas mobile	29
Christmas crafts	31

OXFORD UNIVERSITY PRESS

Away in a manger

Away in a manger,
No crib for a bed,
The little Lord Jesus
Laid down his sweet head.
The stars in the bright sky
Looked down where he lay,
The little Lord Jesus
Asleep on the hay.

Find and colour.

baby ☐   manger ☐   hay ☐   star ☐

Match.

Silent night

Silent night.
Holy night.
All is calm.
All is bright.
Round yon virgin mother and child,
Holy infant so tender and mild.
Sleep in heavenly peace.
Sleep in heavenly peace.

Find and circle.

king shepherd sheep angel star
Joseph Mary Jesus

```
s j o s e p h a
h m p r i w k n
e a l s t a r g
p r j r a h o e
h y e d j p e l
e b s c m t d r
r q u l k i n g
d h s h e e p r
```

Write.

_ _ _ _   _ _ _ _ _ _ _ _   _ _ _ _ _   _ _ _ _

_ _ _ _   _ _ _ _ _   _ _ _ _ _   _ _ _ _ _ _

Rudolph the red-nosed reindeer

Rudolph the red-nosed reindeer
Had a very shiny nose,
And if you ever saw it
You would even say it glows.

All of the other reindeer
Used to laugh and call him names.
They never let poor Rudolph
Join in any reindeer games.

Then one foggy Christmas Eve
Santa came to say,
"Rudolph, with your nose so bright,
Won't you guide my sleigh tonight?"

Then how the reindeer loved him,
As they shouted out with glee,
"Rudolph the red-nosed reindeer
You'll go down in history!"

Number.

Write and circle.

When Santa got stuck up the chimney

When Santa got stuck up the chimney
He began to shout,
"You girls and boys won't get any toys
If you don't pull me out!
My beard is black,
There's soot in my sack,
My nose is tickly too!"
When Santa got stuck up the chimney,
Atchoo! Atchoo! Atchoo!

A Write.

a computer
a book
a football
a doll

Dear _____,
How are you?
For Christmas please may I have a 📗 _____, a _____, and a _____.
Thank you!
Happy Christmas!
Love from _____

a plane
a bicycle
a paintbox
a dress

Stick.

11

O Christmas tree!

O Christmas tree! O Christmas tree!
How lovely are your branches.
O Christmas tree! O Christmas tree!
How lovely are your branches.
Lovely and green they always grow,
Through summer sun and winter snow.
O Christmas tree! O Christmas tree!
How lovely are your branches.

Colour and count.

presents ☐ candles ☐ stars ☐

cards ☐ stockings ☐ bells ☐

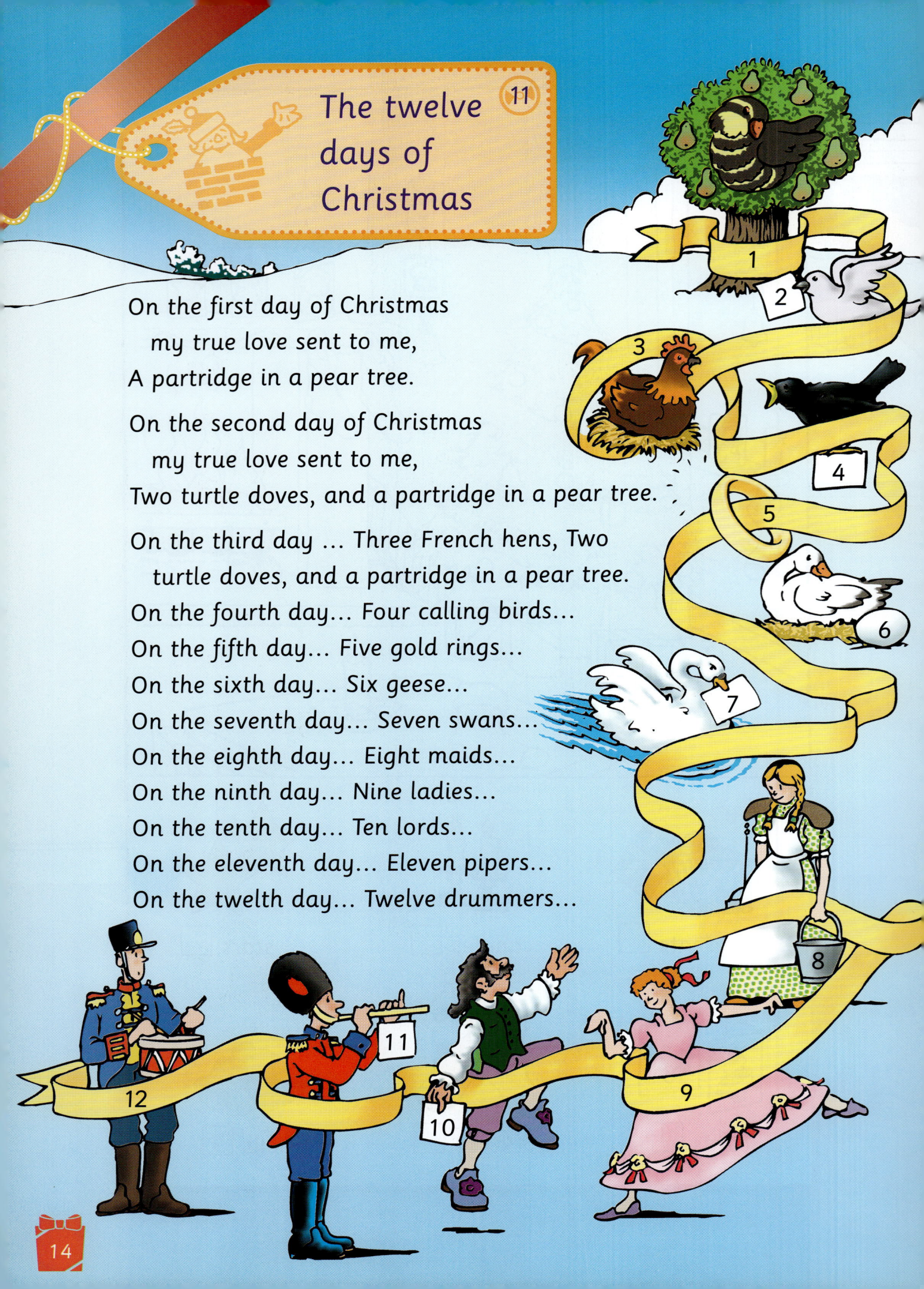

The twelve days of Christmas

On the first day of Christmas
   my true love sent to me,
A partridge in a pear tree.

On the second day of Christmas
   my true love sent to me,
Two turtle doves, and a partridge in a pear tree.

On the third day … Three French hens, Two
   turtle doves, and a partridge in a pear tree.
On the fourth day… Four calling birds…
On the fifth day… Five gold rings…
On the sixth day… Six geese…
On the seventh day… Seven swans…
On the eighth day… Eight maids…
On the ninth day… Nine ladies…
On the tenth day… Ten lords…
On the eleventh day… Eleven pipers…
On the twelfth day… Twelve drummers…

4 Number.

☐ swans a-swimming

☐ maids a-milking

☐ gold rings

☐ French hens

☐ drummers drumming

☐ lords a-leaping

☐ ladies dancing

☐ turtle doves

☐ calling birds

☐ geese a-laying

☐ pipers piping

☐ partridge

We three kings

We three kings of Orient are.
Bearing gifts we travel afar.
Field and fountain, moor and mountain,
Following yonder star.

O star of wonder, star of night,
Star with royal beauty bright.
Westward leading, still proceeding,
Guide us to thy perfect light.

Stickers for page 10–11

© Oxford University Press

Stickers for page 20–21

© Oxford University Press

Help the kings find the stable.

Count, write, and colour.

shepherds ☐   gifts ☐   kings ☐

Frosty the snowman

Frosty the snowman was a jolly happy soul,
With a corncob pipe and a carrot nose,
And two eyes made out of coal.
Frosty the snowman is a fairy tale, they say.
He was made of snow but the children know
How he came to life one day.
There must have been some magic in that
Old silk hat they found,
For when they put it on his head
He began to dance around!

O, Frosty the snowman,
Was alive as he could be!
And the children say he could
Laugh and play
Just the same as you and me.
Thumpety thump thump,
Thumpety thump thump,
Look at Frosty go!
Thumpety thump thump,
Thumpety thump thump,
Over the hills of snow...

Colour.

1 **red**	4 **yellow**	7 **green**
2 **blue**	5 **black**	8 **pink**
3 **orange**	6 **brown**	9 **purple**

Stick.

21

Picture Dictionary

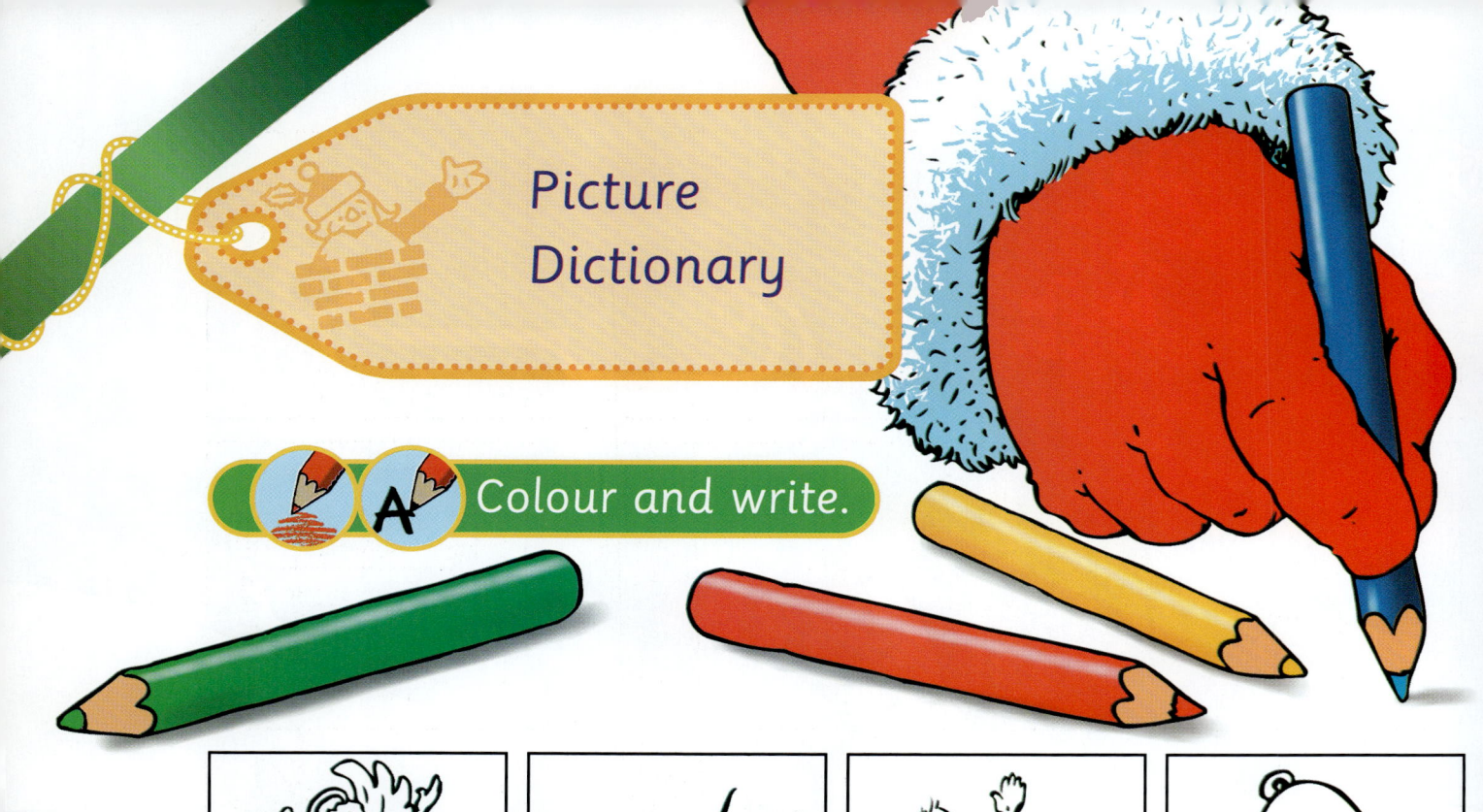

Colour and write.

angel	arm	baby	bell
bicycle	book	boots	buttons
candle	card	chimney	computer
cow	doll	donkey	dress

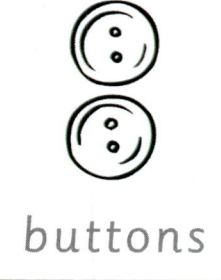

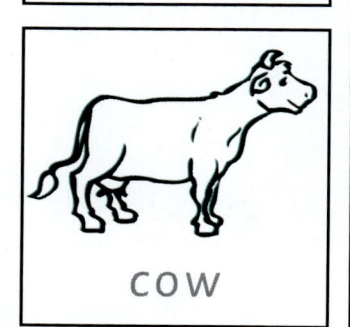

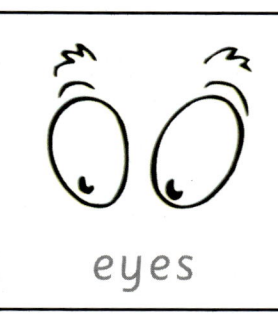

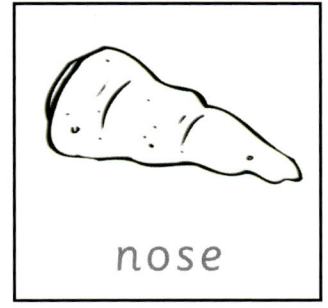

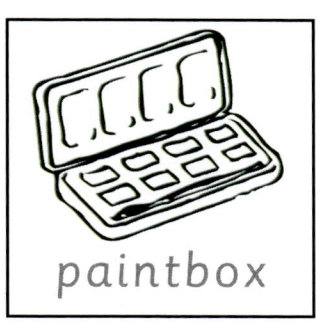

eyes	football	hat	hay
Jesus	Joseph	king	manger
Mary	nose	paintbox	plane
present	reindeer	Santa	sheep
shepherd	sleigh	snowballs	snowman
stable	star	stocking	tree

Answers

P3 Match.

P5 Find and circle.

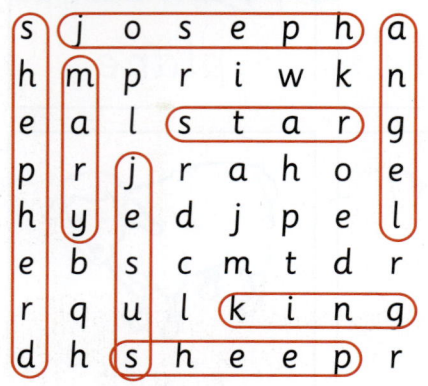

P5 Write.
star; shepherd; sheep; Mary; king; angel; Jesus; Joseph

P7 Number.

P7 Write and circle.

P9 Write.
Dear *Santa*, How are you? For Christmas, please may I have a *book*, a …, and a …
(individual answers)

P13 Count.
presents – 7; candles – 3; stars – 7; cards – 6; stockings - 4; bells – 5

P15 Number.
7 swans a-swimming; 8 maids a-milking; 5 gold rings; 3 French hens; 12 drummers drumming; 10 lords a-leaping; 9 ladies dancing; 2 turtle doves; 4 calling birds; 6 geese a-laying; 11 pipers piping; 1 partridge

P17 Help the kings find the stable.

P17 Count, write and colour.
4 shepherds; 3 gifts; 3 kings

Make the jigsaw.

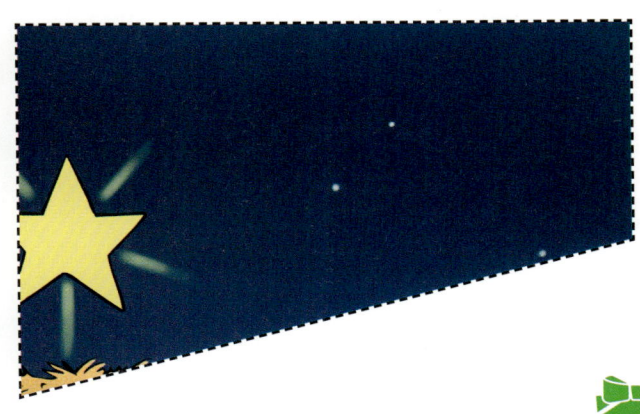

25

Make a pop-up card.

Stick   Stick

Stick   Stick

Fold   Fold   Fold

Happy Christmas!

Photocopiable © Oxford University Press

Make a Christmas mobile.

Photocopiable © Oxford University Press

Make a snowman chain.

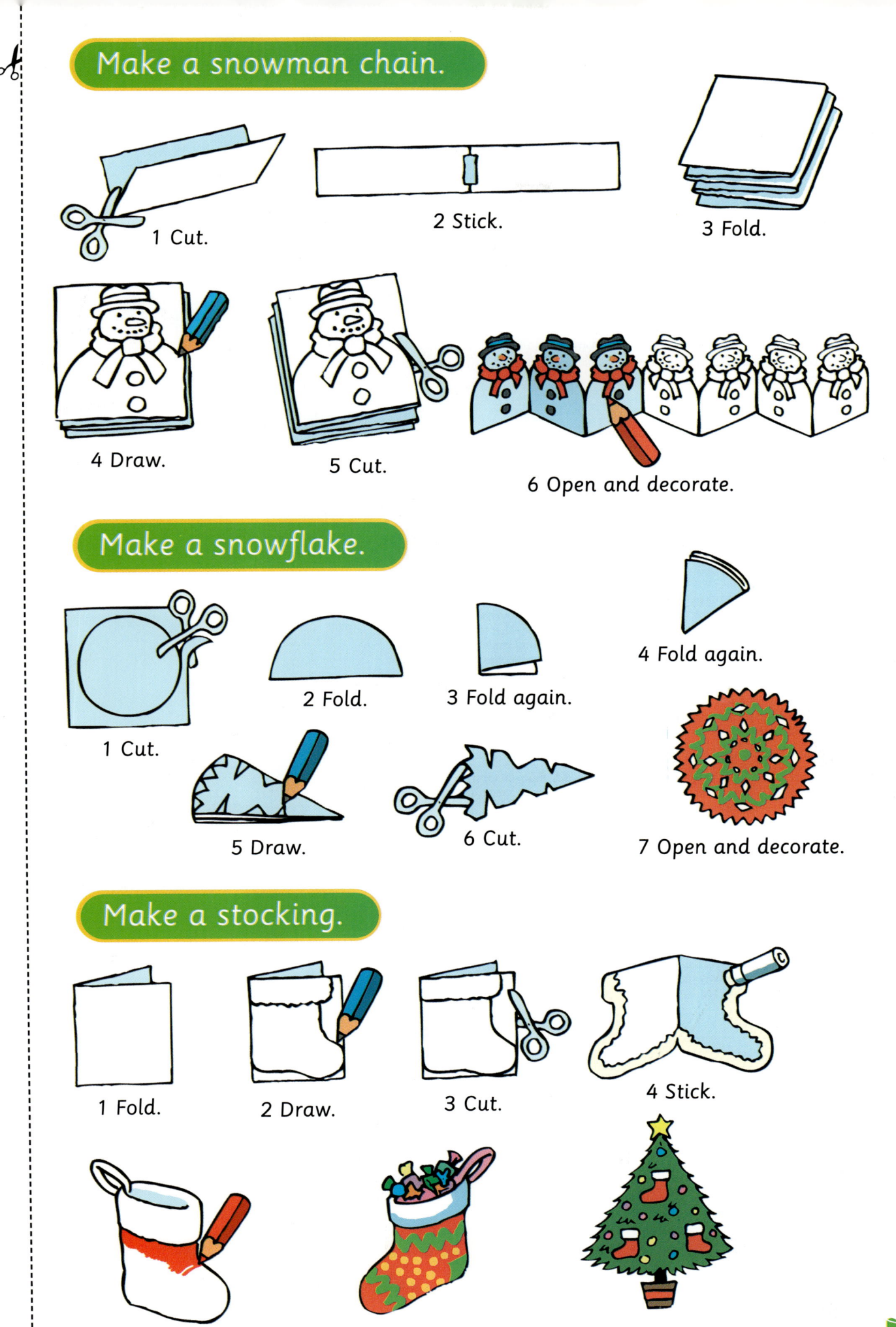

1 Cut.   2 Stick.   3 Fold.

4 Draw.   5 Cut.   6 Open and decorate.

Make a snowflake.

1 Cut.   2 Fold.   3 Fold again.   4 Fold again.

5 Draw.   6 Cut.   7 Open and decorate.

Make a stocking.

1 Fold.   2 Draw.   3 Cut.   4 Stick.

5 Decorate.

Photocopiable © Oxford University Press

OXFORD
UNIVERSITY PRESS

Great Clarendon Street, Oxford OX2 6DP

Oxford University Press is a department of the University of Oxford.
It furthers the University's objective of excellence in research, scholarship,
and education by publishing worldwide in

Oxford   New York

Auckland   Bangkok   Buenos Aires   Cape Town   Chennai
Dar es Salaam   Delhi   Hong Kong   Istanbul   Karachi   Kolkata
Kuala Lumpur   Madrid   Melbourne   Mexico City   Mumbai
Nairobi   São Paulo   Shanghai   Taipei   Tokyo   Toronto

OXFORD and OXFORD ENGLISH are registered trade marks of
Oxford University Press in the UK and in certain other countries

© Oxford University Press 2004

The moral rights of the author have been asserted

Database right Oxford University Press (maker)

First published 2004

2008   2007   2006   2005   2004
10   9   8   7   6   5   4   3   2   1

All rights reserved. No part of this publication may be reproduced,
stored in a retrieval system, or transmitted, in any form or by any means,
without the prior permission in writing of Oxford University Press,
or as expressly permitted by law, or under terms agreed with the appropriate
reprographics rights organization. Enquiries concerning reproduction
outside the scope of the above should be sent to the ELT Rights Department,
Oxford University Press, at the address above

You must not circulate this book in any other binding or cover
and you must impose this same condition on any acquirer

Photocopying

The Publisher grants permission for the photocopying of those pages marked
'photocopiable' according to the following conditions. Individual purchasers
may make copies for their own use or for use by classes that they teach.
School purchasers may make copies for use by staff and students, but this
permission does not extend to additional schools or branches

Under no circumstances may any part of this book be photocopied for resale

Any websites referred to in this publication are in the public domain and
their addresses are provided by Oxford University Press for information only.
Oxford University Press disclaims any responsibility for the content

ISBN 0 19 454604 7

Printed and bound in Spain by Mateu Cromo, S.A. Pinto (Madrid)

ACKNOWLEDGEMENTS

Illustrated by: Robin Edmonds

The authors and publisher are grateful to those who have given permission to reproduce the following extracts and adaptations of copyright material: p18 FROSTY THE SNOWMAN – Words and Music by Steve Nelson and Jack Rollins – © 1950 Unichappell Music Inc - Copyright Renewed – All Rights Reserved – Lyric reproduced by kind permission of Carlin Music Corp., London NW1 8BD; p8 WHEN SANTA GOT STUCK UP THE CHIMNEY © Peer Music (UK) Ltd, London. Reproduced by permission of Peer Music (UK) Ltd. All Rights Reserved; p6 RUDOLPH THE RED-NOSED REINDEER Words and Music by John D. Marks © 1949 Saint-Nicholas Music Publishing Co, USA, Chappell Music Ltd, London W6 8BS. Reproduced by permission of International Music Publications Ltd. All Rights Reserved.